CHRONICLE SERIES

CALGARY

THE STORY AND THE SIGHTS

by

Barry Bondar

In 1800, it was estimated that there were 50 million head of bison roaming the plains of North America. By 1900, only a few animals remained.

FORT CALGARY

IN THE 1860s a new rage was sweeping Europe and North America. People were abandoning the furs of earlier fashion trends in order to possess their own bulky, warm, woolly buffalo robes.

Since there were millions of bison roaming the northern plains, the Hudson's Bay Company looked upon this shift favourably. As profits mounted, however, an unscrupulous breed of independent fur trader began to filter across the border. Their sole objective was to capture as much of the market as quickly as possible through whatever means were necessary.

Although the Hudson's Bay Company was supposedly in control of its vast holdings known as Rupert's Land, the truth was that the area was simply too great for effective management. It was thus a simple matter for the independents to establish themselves in the northern buffalo country. Just outside present-day Lethbridge, Fort Whoop-up rapidly exerted its control over the surrounding countryside. Unlike the giant HBC, the independents were not overly concerned with maintaining reasonable trading relations with the native people, nor with anyone else. One need only examine a note sent by one of the traders to Fort Benton, south of the border, to recognize the cavalier attitudes that prevailed. Beginning with "Dear Friend," the note continues thus: "My partner, Will Geary, got to putting on airs and I shot him and he is dead—the potatoes are looking well. Yours truly, Skookum Jim."

Since profit was the sole driving force of this group, they were willing to do whatever was necessary to entice the native people to trade. Regrettably their most effective bargaining tool was a vile concoction of ingredients which, because it contained a little alcohol, was called "whisky." That the mixture sometimes caused death directly from the additions or from the violence associated with its consumption was unimportant to these men, so long as the whisky stimulated trade.

The rapidly increasing power and authority of the Fort greatly alarmed the government. The many reports of growing lawlessness, of degradation and resultant anger of the native people, and of ever-increasing deaths associated with conflicts between the traders and the Plains tribes were filtering back to Ottawa. It was not until 1869, when Britain formally requested that Canada take over the Hudson's Bay Company lands, that Ottawa had any authority to act. Five years later a contingent of North West Mounted Police entered the Territories in an effort to correct a rapidly deteriorating situation.

Constable of the N.W.M.P. in buffalo coat.

"F" Troop of the N.W.M.P.

At the confluence of the Bow and Elbow rivers the wooden barricades and bunkhouses were hurriedly constructed. Fort Calgary was looked upon as a welcome symbol of government presence and influence by settlers in the surrounding area.

Like a candle to moths the fort rapidly collected a motley assembly of tents and cabins outside its walls. Within two weeks of the fort's construction, the shanty town could even boast of two stores—the I.G. Baker Company of Montana and the Hudson's Bay Company. The lonely N.W.M.P. outpost had suddenly become the territory's social and economic centre.

Fort Whoop-up quickly faded, in part the direct result of the presence of the N.W.M.P., in part a reflection of the disastrous decline of the bison. As a testament to greed the traders had turned the plains into a graveyard. Only a handful of individual animals now ran where once millions had darkened the plains. In turn, the once-proud Plains people were reduced to clinging to the fringes of the invading white society.

With the plummeting trade in buffalo robes both native and white faced an uncertain future. In a desperate attempt to alleviate the ever-increasing threat of starvation, the government looked to the potential of the now empty plains. In 1880 it made a remarkable offer: it would grant leases for up to 40,000 hectares of land for those willing to transform the grasslands into cattle country.

View of Calgary from the Elbow River, 1884. The I.G. Baker & Company store is at left.

CATTLE COUNTRY

Ranches, often thousands of hectares in size, surrounded the young community of Calgary.

THE OFFER OF AN instant empire was one that many wealthy investors and cattle companies simply could not ignore. Not only was the size of the land grant extraordinary, but the Canadian Pacific Railway was already pushing its way west. With access to eastern and western markets soon to be guaranteed, Calgary seemed a most promising venture. It was not long before tens of thousands of cattle could be found on the open prairie. By the time the railway arrived, in 1884, well over 600,000 hectares of land had been gobbled up by just forty-one companies.

The ranching country surrounding the village of Calgary was a strange intermixing of cultures. Hard-bitten and cattle-weary American ranch hands, bringing a taste of the U.S. "wild west," looked on in amazement as Canadian owners and managers with strong British ties carried on an elaborate social life.

Social teas were common, as were elegant dinner parties and dances where formal attire was an expected condition of attendance. Sports included two very British activities: polo and fox hunting (except that in Canada's west a coyote replaced the traditional fox). Ranch homes were designed like British estates, and the beginnings of formal Victorian gardens were established in the vast expanses of the almost treeless prairies.

The cultured atmosphere of the range land was decidedly less well established in the early community of Calgary. Fueled by a steady stream of transient prospectors and miners on the way to their "fortunes" in the mountains to the west, Calgary was best characterized as an oasis of bars, bordellos, bath-houses, and billiard rooms, where high prices prevailed.

Calgary, looking southwest, 1889. The fireball (centre) was built in 1887.

Branding cattle on D.P. MacDonald's ranch, west of Calgary, ca. 1905.

Despite the robust economy and ribald atmosphere of the town, Calgary had some problems which both the government and the Canadian Pacific Railway recognized as dangerous to the new community. The development of cattle country had proven successful, perhaps too successful. So much land was tied up in so few hands that Calgary was threatened with a stunting of its growth even before growth was truly underway. For the sake of both the government and the economically fragile new railway, a well-populated west was required to ensure markets and stability. Stringent laws which limited the amount of land that any single landowner could possess were swiftly enacted in order to promote the development of smaller grain farms.

The early promotions failed. Calgary was first and foremost equated with cattle, and most potential grain farmers were not attracted to the region. Furthermore, those brave souls who attempted to break the soil around Calgary were crushed by a terrible drought in 1890. As if in confirmation of the title of "ranching capital of the west" the town was reduced to importing $85,000.00 worth of flour in 1892 just to supply the local residents.

In the absence of any new economic force the C.P.R. and the established ranching community held inordinate power in the new town. Virtually all money required for real estate development and for the establishment of manufacturing industries flowed directly from these sources.

Of particular value to Calgary was its central location. In 1891 and 1894, spur lines were built to link Calgary with Edmonton and Fort MacLeod. The town's importance grew again in 1897 when an additional railway line was constructed to the Crow's Nest Pass coal mines and the Kootenay mining frenzy. Early Calgary was thus permitted the luxury of slow and steady growth as it consolidated its position as the most important distribution centre for southern Alberta and British Columbia.

Haying, ca. 1893.

Preparing the fields, 1917.

SETTLERS

WITH THE START of the new century, the town was inundated with settlers. The latest of the land promotions had proven to be enormously successful, and people from around the world flocked to the town where grand dreams were said to come true.

"I am the Great Alberta," proclaimed an advertisement in *The Calgary Herald*, "The Empire of Fulfilment...The land where the opportunities are unlimited and the climate ideal. I am prosperity to him who would enter my gates; my storehouses are full and overflowing..."

Reality, of course, was somewhat less ideal than these brash promises would suggest. Still, the promises were believed, and thousands of settlers willingly accepted a difficult beginning in order to create for themselves a better future. Most of the new arrivals lived in small sod houses and many were reduced to the collection of bison bones in order to earn a little money to pay debts. The great slaughter of these animals had spurred the creation of a new industry—bison bones which were ground up as fertilizer. It was said that a single pile of buffalo skulls awaiting shipment to eastern plants represented the remains of 50,000 animals.

The greater the number of immigrants who set out for Calgary, the greater the lure for others contemplating the journey. The process of promotion, immigration, and more promotion built on itself until there was a steady stream of new arrivals seeking prosperity in the west. Agriculture soared. Whereas only 32,000 hectares of land were under cultivation in 1898, that figure ballooned to 1.3 million by 1910. Livestock found a robust competitor in grains.

This massive influx of people also gave Calgary a distinctive European influence. By 1911 well over half of the population was foreign-born, and the city rang with dozens of languages, including German, Hungarian, Italian, Ukrainian, French and Austrian.

Buffalo skulls in front of sod house, 1910. Bison bones were collected and sold for fertilizer.

THE SANDSTONE CITY

A SPECULATIVE fever began to build, and by 1910 the city had gone quite mad. Land prices skyrocketed and lots could change hands several times in a matter of hours, always at a profit. Whenever the fever showed signs of abating, another piece of news would force the temperature even higher. First, there was the rumour that two additional transcontinental railways would be constructed. The frenzy built. Next came word that the C. P. R. would locate its repair shops for the entire region in Calgary. The prices soared still higher. Rumours of a gold strike just west of the city... higher yet. Any piece of good news, even if only fragmentary and unfounded, was sufficient to fuel the fire.

Almost overnight Calgary's original handful of wealthy individuals was swamped by the millionaires created by the real estate boom. Since money alone was apparently sufficient for entry into the upper class, there was a clamour by the newly wealthy to establish exclusive districts catering to those of wealth.

Calgary had been notorious for being unable to enforce building restrictions and planning guidelines. As a result, early Calgary had seen a mixing of

Looking east on 8th Avenue from Centre Street.

income levels and social status throughout the city. For the first time, however, there was a demand for a clear separation of the elite. The most successful of the bastions of the wealthy was the very strictly controlled subdivision of Mount Royal, owned and developed by the C.P.R.'s real estate arm. Exclusiveness was jealously guarded by residents.

Calgary's transformation was so rapid that by 1913 people were forced to live in tents until accommodations could be constructed. The city skyline grew at an extraordinary pace, and a once humble shanty town of wooden buildings took on an air of distinguished permanence.

Turn-of-the-century Calgary was a uniquely beautiful city. Using local dusky-coloured sandstones, the city's stonemasons, now the highest paid workers in the city, were able to create a city core that was characterized by a sense of stability and strength. With only a few exceptions, the buildings were required to remain at a maximum height of six floors. Firefighting equipment could not handle anything higher. As a result, Calgary's centre had a consistency of design and construction materials that was to make it one of the most distinctive of western cities.

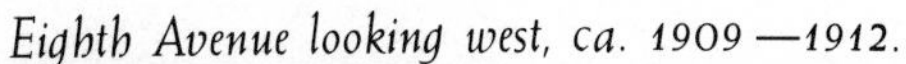

Eighth Avenue looking west, ca. 1909 —1912.

Mount Royal district of Calgary—a C.P.R. real estate development designed for the wealthy.

Eighth Avenue looking east, ca. 1909—1912.

The C.P.R. Palliser Hotel, 9th Avenue, ca. 1930.

Although Calgary had a number of well-established businesses such as the Burns stockyards and abattoirs, and the Calgary Brewing and Malting Company, it was real estate that fueled the city's growth. One of the favourite tools of the real estate promoters was streetcars. Every effort was made to ensure that streetcar lines were extended to parcels of property held by the speculators, as these transportation lines were necessary to lure buyers. Some speculators even constructed their own lines and then donated them to the city.

The easy availability of streetcars allowed Calgary a rapid outward expansion, a characteristic which has persisted till the present day. One of the early lines, which was long considered to be a "white elephant," was the Bowness car line. The area it serviced never became a popular residential site, and the Bowness line was reduced to carrying milk from dairies to the city.

During this period of rapid growth, Calgary was the most dynamic and powerful city in the region. When the federal government contemplated creating a new province called Alberta, in 1905, Calgarians presumed that their city would be the capital. They were in for a rude awakening.

For many years the northern community of Edmonton had watched, with considerable frustration, the dynamic growth of its southern neighbour. Edmonton citizens remembered well those exciting days when it was their community which awaited the arrival of the C.P.R. Originally slated to pass through the more northern Yellowhead Pass and thus through Edmonton, the route of the C.P.R. had subsequently been shifted south. Though there were sound economic reasons for the change in the route, Edmonton still smarted from the loss.

Now it was time to choose a provincial capital. Edmonton lobbied hard for the privilege of being the capital city. In 1905 the city was awarded the title temporarily, and one year later, despite presentations by many other Alberta communities, it was made permanent. The longstanding rivalry between Edmonton and Calgary was not mitigated by Edmonton's victory; in fact, it exists today, in a friendly fashion, and both cities nurture their competitive spirits.

In 1914 Calgary was astounded by the discovery of oil in Turner Valley. Though it was not realized at the time, the discovery was to signal the last gasp of the boom years.

Real estate speculators now considered themselves oilmen. Literally hundreds of companies were formed, and people milled around newly opened offices in order to capture a piece of the action. Over 85 million dollars of capital was raised from the sale of stocks. Everyone expected that their company would be the first to locate the "gusher" that would continue this wonderful explosion of growth.

Turner Valley proved most disappointing: despite the scores of wells the huge pools of crude could not be located. Though the first find would be an important symbol for the future, it would be a far distant future. For the next several decades Calgary would suffer... the boom was over, the general trend was down.

Investors waiting to buy oil stocks, May 15, 1914. The speculative fever surrounding the discovery of oil was representative of the early decades of rapid, dynamic growth.

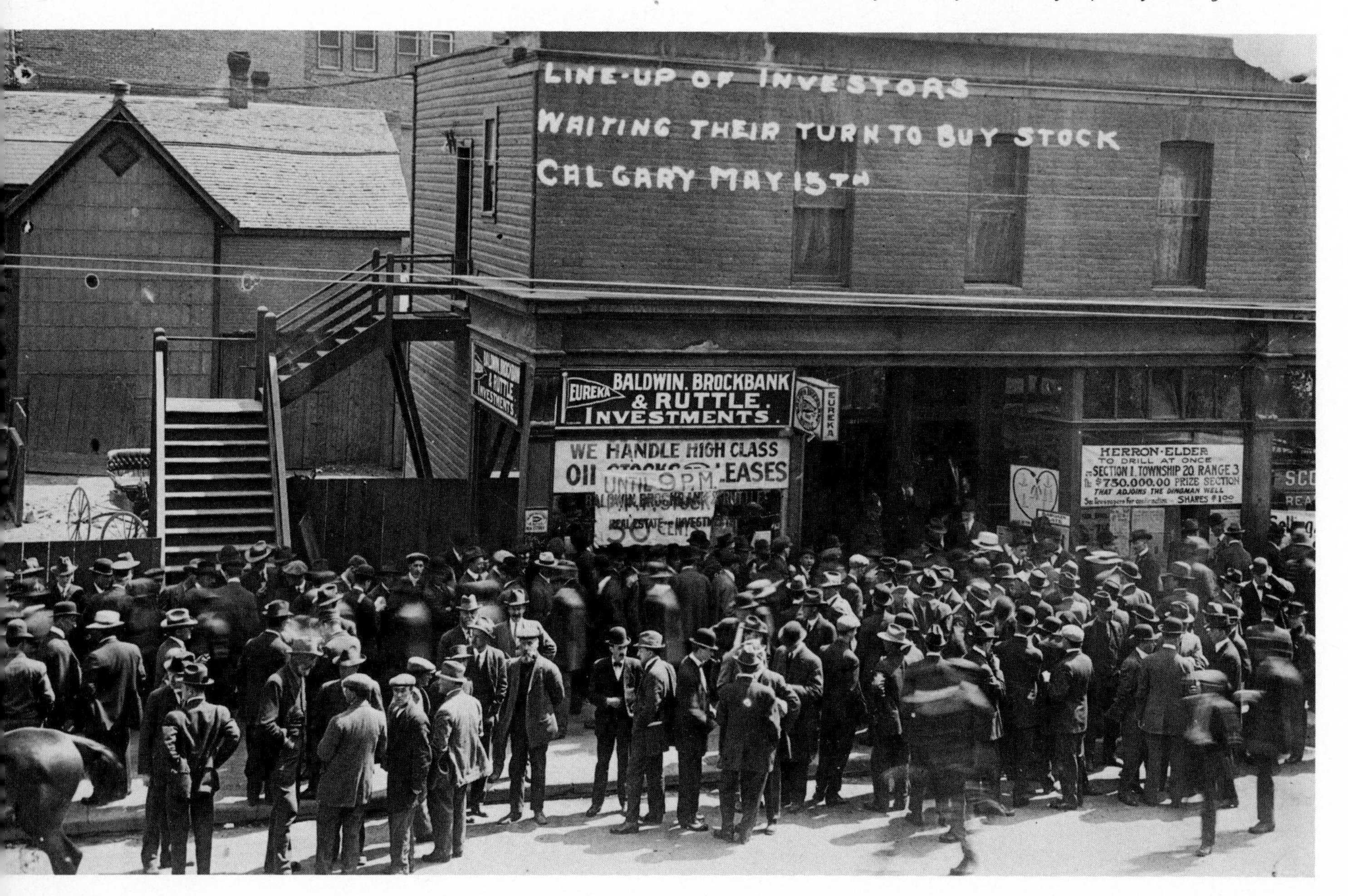

HARDSHIPS

FROM 1914 TO THE 1940s, Calgary would suffer a roller coaster ride of ups and downs with a very clear emphasis on the downs. Markets were declining or disappearing; competition was increasing. Once-stable industries were rapidly finding themselves "pushed to the wall." Long-time residents wistfully remembered the excitement and the dreams that had been spawned in those hectic years at the turn of the century. Now, every slight improvement, every good year in the grain or cattle industry seemed only to tease the citizens before hopes for improvement were dashed once again.

Hope seemed nothing more than a cruel joke when the very climate seemed to turn against the land and its people during the thirties. Farmers suffered years of being dried out, rusted out, blown out, and having their crops decimated by grasshoppers. Dust storms blackened the skies and drifts of soil covered broken fences and idle machinery. Oxen pulled automobiles when there was no money left for gasoline. Thousands of desperate men poured on to trains in search of work—any work, any place, under any conditions, and for whatever wages were offered.

Dust storm, ca. 1930.

Even Calgary's most durable industries staggered under the burden of the depression. The livestock industry, though still centred in Calgary, was barely holding its own. It could not grow at a time when the economy was desperate for growth. Too many factors were beyond its control: markets were unstable, banks were more conservative, and money for expansion was not forthcoming.

When the C.P.R., long an important element in Calgary's success, was forced to close its Ogden repair shops in 1931, it seemed to many citizens that the lifeblood of the city was slowly and painfully being drained away. With some bitterness the city could only look back on the memories of the good years. What great potential the real estate boom and the Turner Valley oil discovery had once offered. What great folly those dreams seemed now.

Still the city struggled on. Occasionally a new manufacturer would open its doors; a few retail stores expanded their facilities; investment and brokerage houses established their provincial offices in the city. Despite the unrelenting troubles, these meagre signs of an improved economy were grasped with an unquenchable faith in the future.

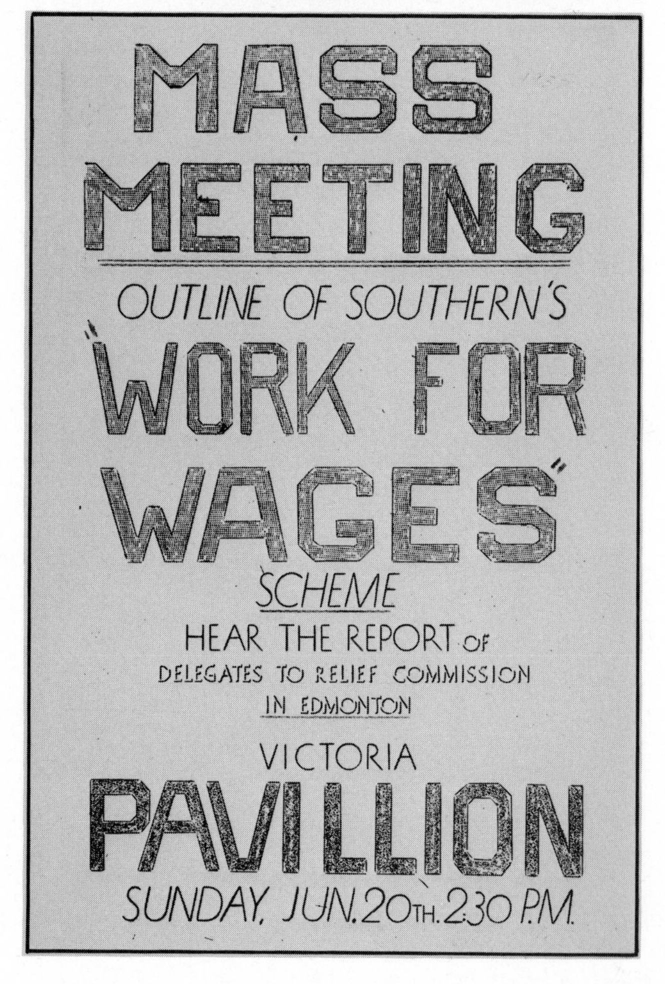

(Upper) Unemployed marching in Calgary, 1935.

(Right) Handbill of a mass meeting of the unemployed, 1937.

(Top) Unemployed waiting to board boxcars during the "Ottawa Trek" of 1935.

(Above) Animals were used to pull automobiles when no money was available to purchase gasoline. These vehicles were nicknamed "Bennett Buggies" after the prime minister of the day, R.B. Bennett.

OIL

ONE BRAVE MAN would not give up on the Turner Valley oilfield. Robert A. Brown, Sr. trusted in a theory that a major pool of oil did indeed exist in the area. Investors were so cynical about Turner Valley, however, that he was forced to mortgage his home, sell his car, and borrow heavily, purely on his unwavering faith in his hunch.

In 1936 Turner Valley Royalties No. 1 blew in. With this new and larger discovery, hope bubbled to the surface of Calgary once again. Oil just might be the means of returning the city to the heady boom times.

But another decade of frustration followed. Dry holes or poor producers were all that were located. While these limited discoveries helped support Calgary's improving economy, and while they placed Calgary as western Canada's oil centre, the discoveries were not of the international magnitude required for prosperity. Turner Valley seemed nothing more than a cruel, taunting spectre. Its mere presence was an enticement to which many succumbed. Exploration continued, defeat followed.

Then, in 1947, just outside the community of Leduc, a single well blew in with terrifying ferocity. So huge was this pool of black gold that the night sky was ablaze with the scores of flares used to burn off excess gas and spur the movement of oil to the surface. Exploration and drilling companies stampeded to the new bonanza. With each new discovery, Calgary's position as a major world oil capital was strengthened. The boom had returned with a vengeance.

As if in an effort to remove virtually all traces of the short-lived boom of the early 1900s, skyscrapers of steel and glass engulfed the sandstone city. Calgary focused upon its great future, and with much of its past falling beneath the bulldozers, Calgary took on the bright, vibrant appearance of a youthful city. The skyline mushroomed into a field of towering highrise buildings. Its expanding city boundaries rapidly swallowed much of the surrounding farmland—which had been the impetus for the first great rush to prosperity.

Today Calgary retains its traditional economic foundation of cattle and grain, but petroleum has taken the leading role in driving the city forward. The dramatic skyscrapers of the major oil companies in the downtown core are mute testament to this

(Right) South end of the Turner Valley oilfield, ca. 1930s.
(Far right) A "gusher" in the Turner Valley field, ca. 1930s.

fact. Although most of the city's older buildings have been replaced, Calgary refuses to abandon totally the traditions of its western frontier origin. The exuberance of the wild west is always just below the surface.

The journey from cattle country to international oil centre has been long and fraught with many difficulties. Still, the city has never abandoned its optimism nor its drive and ambition. Those qualities remain as integral to the character of the city as the yearly Calgary Stampede.

The faces of Calgary: top, 1883, bottom, 1912, opposite top, ca. 1930, bottom, 1968.

THE CALGARY STAMPEDE

WITH THE INTRODUCTION of successful grain farming, the traditional patterns of the open range began to fade slowly from the west. For those who had spent their lives tending the vast, drifting cattle herds, the loss of this way of life was a difficult and sad period of transition. The skills of riding, roping, and branding which represented a lifetime of careful development were growing more and more useless in a country increasingly fragmented by fences.

Yet even as the ways of the old west were disappearing, public interest in the life of the cowboy increased dramatically. "Wild West" shows and cowboy movies proliferated, but many became almost side-show parodies of an honourable way of life. Still, the mere presence of these shows helped preserve at least fragments of a historical phase.

Mr. Guy Weadick was one man who wished to see the creation of a large western show that would translate the skills of legitimate cowboys into a more competitive and entertaining vehicle for the public. He had spent his entire life as a range hand and had been involved in many western shows as cattle country faded. He wished to transfer his love of a way of life to an ongoing western extravaganza that would celebrate, rather than parody, the life of this independent breed.

Weadick looked to Calgary as a potential home for his grand scheme. Fortunately he was able to convince four of the city's earliest and now wealthiest pioneers of the potential of such a dream. Having made their fortunes from cattle country, they now wanted some of their old way of life to be reflected in a new and vibrant way. Using $100,000 offered by the "Big Four" as they were later called, Weadick created the first Calgary Stampede in 1912. Others followed in 1919 and 1923. So successful were these events that the Stampede became a regular yearly event in 1924.

By the time Weadick left the Stampede in 1932, it had been transformed into the biggest western outdoor show in North America. Admittedly, the participants were now less ranch hands than they were professional athletes. Still, the skills used in their competitions were the very skills that Weadick hoped would be forever preserved as a testimony to a vanishing way of life.

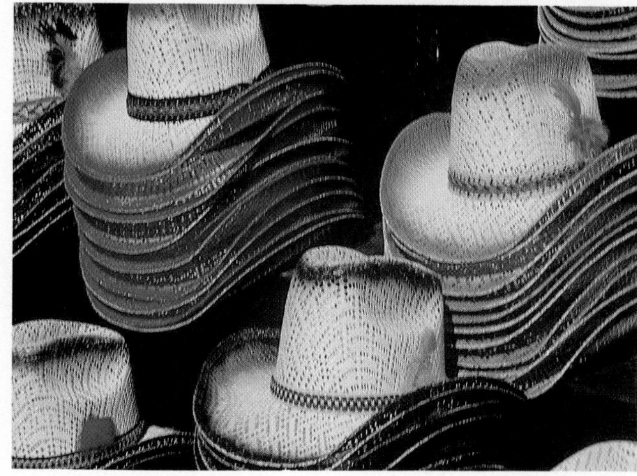

29

The Calgary Stampede, the largest rodeo event in North America, continues to keep alive the skills of riding, roping, and steer wrestling that were an essential part of life on the range during the early years of the cattle empires.

10
11
12

DOWNTOWN

THE TRANSFORMATION of Calgary's central core over the last few decades has been truly remarkable. Long-time residents shake their heads in amazement at the changes that have been wrought since the huge oil boom of the 1970s.

The difficult decades from 1914 through to the 1950s had the effect of preserving intact virtually all the old sandstone city in the central core. Residents were quite accustomed to strolling past these short, squat, brown grey buildings whose gargoyles, carved from sandstone blocks, stared impassively down upon the passers-by. Highrises were rare, even in the 1960s. In 1967, the entire city celebrated as the Calgary Tower was raised foot by foot in a process of continuous concrete pouring. At 190 metres, the Tower dominated the skyline and was a source of pride for the entire community. One need only look to the buildings which now dwarf the Tower to understand the magnitude of change in the last several years.

During this period of dramatic change much of the old city was reduced to rubble. Fortunately, many of the original sandstone structures have been preserved along Stephen Avenue Mall (Eighth Avenue). This offers a delightful walking tour where the flavour of turn-of-the-century Calgary can be experienced.

For the most part, however, Calgary's core is a reflection of modern architecture, sculpture, and gardens. From the massive brown marble Petro-Canada building to the blue tint of the new city hall, Calgary's appearance is now one of a vibrant new city with its eye on the future.

The ever increasing amenities of the downtown area, such as the Calgary Centre for the Performing Arts, are also attracting greater all-round use of the central core. For many years Calgarians looked upon "downtown" as the business hub of the community. The recent massive expansion, however, is luring a greater number of restaurants, theatres, and night spots back to the city centre, creating an active, dynamic union of cultural and business activities.

Within the maze of massive office towers and apartment buildings are many hidden treasures that bring the human element back to what can often become an impersonal environment of concrete. In addition to several outdoor parks, the one-hectare climatically controlled Devonian Gardens offer a natural paradise whatever the weather may be outside. Dramatic sculptures, such as *Brotherhood of Man* and *The Conversation,* are becoming increasingly common as the city slowly begins to assimilate the effects of its rapid growth and transform a once quiet regional city into the international oil centre it has become.

The Calgary Tower.

The oil boom of recent years stimulated the investment of billions of dollars in the city. This is most clearly seen in the downtown core, where a dramatic increase in highrise and office towers has surrounded and dwarfed the Calgary Tower—once the tallest structure in the city.

Opposite, lower: The old city hall reflected in the gleaming windows of the new city hall poignantly underlines the city's changes.

D.E.BLACK
STORE

EXPLORING CALGARY'S HERITAGE

This page and opposite: Heritage Park.

CALGARY HAS MADE a conscious effort to preserve as much as possible of its proud past. A 16-hectare prairie park, for instance, has been set aside to ensure that the site of the original N.W.M.P. fort is preserved as a reminder of Calgary's beginnings. Indeed, virtually every phase of Calgary's evolution has been preserved in some manner.

The age of cattle country has been protected not only in the Calgary Stampede but also through the preservation of the old Bow Valley Ranch House, located in Fish Creek Provincial Park. Built in 1896, this magnificent home reflects the British influence which tamed Canada's "wild west." A nearby Visitors' Centre traces the history of the city and its early settlers.

By far the best known of Calgary's historical centres is the 25.5-hectare Heritage Park. Dozens of representative buildings from the turn of the century have been collected at the site to provide an exciting glimpse into the early life of Alberta. From the bakery with its operating stone ovens to the blacksmith shop and the dining room of the grand old Wainwright Hotel, Heritage Park makes the early years come alive. Visitors are offered the opportunity to experience a steam-driven train, an electric streetcar, and the S.S. *Moyie* paddlewheeler, which takes tours on the Glenmore Reservoir.

The city also has more than a dozen museums which trace virtually every aspect of Calgary's past. Some, like the Stockmen's Memorial Foundation and the Sarcee People's Museum, provide detailed accounts of specific aspects of the early years. Others, such as the world-famous Glenbow Museum, can better offer an overview of the story of Calgary and of the province.

Heritage Park is a "living museum," where visitors can reexperience historic times.

Not every aspect of Calgary's history remains locked in museums or parks. Some elements of the city's story remain in active use by the residents. Such is the case with two of the most distinctive subdivisions of the city, Mount Royal and Inglewood.

Inglewood is located just east of the confluence of the Bow and Elbow rivers. When it was speculated that this would be the area of the main station of the C. P. R., many early residents purchased land in anticipation of major profits which would arise from close proximity to the railway terminal. As it turned out, the railway moved further west. Still, many of the most prominent of the early citizens remained in the area, and the venerable old homes reflect the pattern of life for those of affluence during the late 1800s.

Built and controlled by the C. P. R., Mount Royal was established during the real estate boom of the first decade of the twentieth century. Fueled by the huge influx of immigrants to the city in search of land and prosperity, this early boom created a multitude of instant millionaires that clamoured for their own exclusive district. The C. P. R. happily obliged.

Although there has been a rapid growth of new suburbs in recent years, Calgarians are careful to preserve older communities.

THE CALGARY ZOO AND PREHISTORIC PARK

ESTABLISHED IN 1920 on St. George's Island, the Calgary Zoo has been undergoing major renovations over the last decade. What was once a traditional assemblage of bars and sterile cages has now been transformed into an exciting facility where the stress is on natural environment for the captive animals. The success of this transformation, reflected in the dramatic increase in births of many of the species, has catapulted Calgary into the forefront of an international movement to protect breeding stock of endangered species. Represented here are many wild populations which are suffering disastrous declines, due to the rapid disappearance of their natural habitats.

With many kilometres of wooded pathways, dozens of exhibits, and a wealth of gardens and conservatories, Calgary Zoo invites a most pleasurable visit.

The 2.6-hectare Prehistoric Park is a striking re-creation of the Mesozoic era spanning a period of 230 million to 65 million years ago. Life-size replicas of dinosaurs are combined with fascinating geological landscapes to bring to life a time when dinosaurs ruled Alberta. The outstanding quality and creativity of this huge exhibit clearly deserves its international reputation.

Calgary Zoo, and Conservatory.

PARKS AND GARDENS

CALGARY'S EXTRAORDINARY growth over the last few years has caused a rapid expansion of housing subdivisions into outlying areas. The fact that so much of the city is new gives the initial impression of a community with a dearth of green space. This first impression is indeed deceiving. Calgary possesses some spectacular park areas which citizens enjoy to the fullest.

The Bow River is the focal point for many of these pockets of beautifully landscaped or natural regions. Prince's Island Park, located only a few minutes from the downtown core, is used regularly by business people as a place to escape for a relaxing lunch or to use the jogging or walking trails. Just east of this landscaped oasis there are regions of natural rather than landscaped beauty. St. Patrick's Island Park, for example, is connected by a footbridge to the 16 hectares of natural grasses at the site of Fort Calgary. The Sam Livingston Fish Hatchery, which produces 8.6 million fish for Alberta's lakes and rivers, is a combination of natural and landscaped vegetation. Open to the public, it is used regularly as a picnic area. For those interested in natural history, the Inglewood Bird Sanctuary is a quiet and peaceful pocket of forest and tangled brush which shelters a multitude of different bird species.

Calgary's tradition has been one of believing in large dreams and developing large schemes, and the size of many of the city's parks seems to reflect this attitude. One need only consider the scale of Glenmore Park and Reservoir area in the southern part of the city. A pathway rings the entire reservoir and offers spectacular views of the Elbow River Valley and the man-made lake. Weaselhead Flats, the wilderness extension of the Glenmore Parklands, extends westward to the Sarcee Indian Reserve. This untouched natural environment grants spectacular views of the Rocky Mountains and is a perfect spot for those who enjoy the quiet solitude of exploration in a forested area, where deer and red-tailed hawks are still regularly sighted.

Also to the south is the Fish Creek Provincial Park, used as both a wildlife refuge within the city boundaries and as a major recreation area. Fish Creek

Glenmore Park.

Fish Creek Provincial Park.

has facilities ranging from miles of cycling paths to swimming facilities at the lake and an equestrian centre. It is also very popular in winter for cross-country skiing and snowshoeing.

The Nose Hill Park, in contrast, is a huge open grassland escarpment in the north of the city which offers spectacular views of the city and mountains, and a glimpse into the natural world of the prairies. To explore this grassland area is to begin to understand the bonds that can develop between farmers and ranchers and their land. This bond remains a strong element in Calgary's ongoing drive to preserve the traditions of its rural origins.

Finally, Bowness Park at the western edge of the city is a recreational haven for the community. A huge lagoon is used for boating in the summer and as a natural skating rink in the winter.

As these and many other park areas attest, Calgarians remain concerned about creating a balance between cultural, recreational, landscaped and wilderness areas.

ROYAL BANK
EATONS

Peyto Lake, Banff National Park.

IN THE CENTRE OF THINGS

CALGARIANS TAKE great pride in being in the centre of things. This extends not only to business and political affairs but also to the physical location of the city. In fact, it was Calgary's central location which helped convince the C. P. R. to send its tracks past Fort Calgary, thereby ensuring the survival of a young community.

Today Calgary is central to some of the most breathtaking wilderness, scenic, and recreational areas of Canada. To the west are Banff National Park and Kananaskis Provincial Park.

The 6,594 square kilometres of Banff National Park has recently been designated as a world heritage site by the United Nations. The rugged wilderness splendour of the Front and Main ranges makes this selection a fitting contribution to the world's recognized natural treasures. Recently celebrating its hundredth anniversary, Banff National Park grew from a small reserve centred around a few thermal hot springs to become the centrepiece of a national system of parks recognized as one of the finest in the world.

The 4,000-square kilometre Kananaskis Country is a recent provincial contribution to the concept of preservation of wilderness areas. Providing world class skiing, golfing, and other recreational pursuits within a wilderness setting, Kananaskis Country is a year round, well-balanced centre for the entire province. Calgarians are fortunate in that it requires but a brief scenic drive to enter this mountain paradise.

To the south is another of Canada's national parks, Waterton Lakes. Nestled in the extreme southwestern corner of Alberta, Waterton is a lesser known cousin to Banff, yet its scenery rivals that of any area in the world. This is a truly unique natural landscape produced when a huge sheet of stone was thrust up and over the foothills during the process of

The Red Deer River Valley near Drumheller.

mountain building. As a result, prairie grasses abruptly meet a spectacular mountain front. Because of unique climatic conditions, Waterton houses some of the most striking natural floral gardens in the province.

Finally, to the east are the arid badlands of "Dinosaur Country." The strange configurations of the "hoodoos" of the Red Deer River Valley, formed by erosion, are the perfect other-worldly backdrop to one of the world's greatest collections of dinosaur bones. The town of Drumheller proudly offers the recently constructed Tyrrell Museum of Paleontology, through which visitors can explore this most fascinating fossil resource. Dinosaur Provincial Park, some 50 kilometres from the town of Brooks, also has the distinction of being a UNESCO World Heritage Site.

Hoodoos, formed by wind and water erosion.

Kananaskis Country.

Canadian Cataloguing in Publication Data

Bondar, Barry.
Calgary chronicles

ISBN 0-920620-98-1

1. Calgary (Alta.) - History. 2. Calgary (Alta.) - Description - Guide-books. 3. Calgary (Alta.) - Description - Views. I. Title.
FC3697.3.B65 1986 917.12'33 C86-091225-6
F1079.5.C35B65 1986

Typeset by The Typeworks, Vancouver, B.C.

Printed by D.W. Friesen & Sons, Altona, Manitoba, Canada

Published by Whitecap Books Ltd., 1086 W. 3rd St., North Vancouver, B.C.

Photo Credits

Front cover: John Burridge, Photo/Graphics

Back cover: Glenbow Museum, NB-16-362

pp. 2—23: Glenbow Museum
p.2: NA-1041-15; p. 3: NA-1161-7; p. 4: NA-659-16; p. 5: NA-1038-1; p. 6: NA-217-28; p. 7: NA-2399-23; p. 8: NA-3522-11; p. 9: NA-381-2; p. 10 top: NA-237-14, bottom: NA-2685-35; p. 11: NA-2520-67; p. 12: NA-16-360; p. 13: NA-1009-11; p. 14 top: NA-1044-1, bottom: NA-3182-20; p. 15: NA-1009-12; p. 16 top: NA-2736-1, bottom: NA-601-1; p. 17: NA-4235-1; p. 18 top: NA-2629-3, bottom: NA-2434-1; p. 19 top: NA-4532-1, bottom: NA-4532-2; p. 20: NA-67-68; p. 21: NA-67-94; p. 22 top: NA-298-2, bottom: NA-2288-1; p. 23 top: NA-2399-33, bottom: NA-2399-44
p. 24/25: John Burridge, Photo/Graphics; pp. 26—28: Travel Alberta; p. 29 top: Carolyn Angus, Photo/Graphics; p. 29 bottom: Travel Alberta: p. 30: John Burridge, Photo/Graphics; pp. 31—38: Travel Alberta; p. 33: Cameron Young; p. 39: Cameron Young; p. 40: Travel Alberta; p. 41: Cameron Young; p. 42/43: John Burridge, Photo/Graphics; p. 44: Gunter Marx, Photo/Graphics; pp. 45—47: Travel Alberta; p. 48: Cameron Young